THINK ABOUT

Being
DEAF

Maggie Woolley

First published in the UK in 1998 by

Belitha Press Limited
London House, Great Eastern Wharf,
Parkgate Road, London SW11 4NQ

Text and illustrations copyright © Belitha Press Limited 1998
Cover design by Kathy Petelinsek

Published in the United States by
Smart Apple Media
123 South Broad Street
Mankato, Minnesota 56001

Library of Congress Cataloging-in-Publication Data

Woolley, Maggie.
Being deaf / Maggie Woolley.
p. cm. — (Think about)
Includes index.
Summary: Examines the nature, causes, history, treatment, means of communication,
challenges, and social aspects of deafness.
ISBN 1-887068-85-6
1. Deafness—Juvenile literature.   2. Deaf—Juvenile literature.   [1. Deaf.   2. Physically
handicapped.]   I. Title.   II. Series: Think about (Mankato, Minn.)

RF291.37.W66   1999
617.8—dc21   98-39970

9 8 7 6 5 4 3 2 1

Photographs by: SPL (Julian Baum, James-King Holmes, Astrid & Hans-Friedler Michler,
Gary Parker, Blaire Seitz, Jim Selby, Jane Shemilt, Laurence Monneret), BBC Education, Getty
Images (Elie Bernager, Zigy Kaluzny, Lawrence Migdale, Anne Nielson, Ron Sangha, Bob
Thomas, Terry Vine, David Young Wolff), Giles Bernard/Photofusion, British Council, British
Museum, E.T. Archive, Beethoven House, Express & Star, Isabelle Foulkes © Deaf Aardvark,
Hearing Dogs for Deaf People, Peter Heimsath/RexFeatures, Collections (Sandra Lousada,
John Wender), Maggie Murray/Format, NASA, North Wind Picture Archives, Nottingham
Group Ltd, Format (Ulrike Preuss, Paula Solloway), RNID, Friends for Young Deaf People,
Sound Seekers, Tate Gallery, Telegraph Colour Library, Carol Weinberg/BMG, WESCO
Front cover photo by Express & Star, Wolverhampton

Words in **bold** are explained in the glossary on pages 30 and 31.

ABOUT THE AUTHOR

Maggie Woolley, who began to go deaf as a child, is a producer and sign language presenter for television programs for hearing-impaired people. She also is the director of an arts charity for deaf and disabled people.

Contents

Understanding deafness

When most people close their eyes and listen, they hear many things. If they tried to make a list of everything they could hear, it would soon be a very long list. There are sounds all around us. Even in very quiet places we can hear such things as insects buzzing, the wind blowing through the trees, or airplanes high in the sky. People who are deaf can't hear these noises. They have to learn different ways of understanding the world of sound.

How many people are deaf?

There are about 250,000 people in the United States who are considered totally deaf. Millions of other people lose their hearing as they grow older; these people are called hard-of-hearing. Sometimes babies are born deaf. Hearing children learn to speak by listening to their parents, family, and friends. It can be difficult for deaf children to learn to speak, however, because they can't hear their own voice or imitate the voices of people around them.

It is often difficult to know if someone is deaf. These deaf children look no different than children with hearing.

Sign language

Some deaf people use a language of their own called **sign language**. Different countries may have their own sign languages. Deaf people from different countries can often communicate with each other because sign languages are easier to learn than spoken or written languages. To talk in sign language, people use hand movements and facial expressions.

> Learning to use sign language can be both fun and useful.

◀ This television program is presented in sign language by a deaf man, helping many deaf people keep in touch with news and events.

Do deaf people miss out?

If we turn off the sound on our favorite television show, we soon become bored and even annoyed because things don't make sense. Most people might think that this means the deaf miss out on enjoying television. But many programs now have **subtitles**—called closed-captioning—so that deaf people can read what is being said. Some programs are presented in sign language by deaf people or have **sign language interpreters** at the side of the screen.

THINK ABOUT

Language

You are always using language. Even if you're sitting quietly on your own, or if you're doing something simple such as tying your shoelaces, you are using language to think. Could you make sense of things or think at all without language? Many deaf people use sign language to have conversations with other people, but they think and dream in sign language too.

What is deafness?

Most deaf people have some hearing; very few are totally deaf. Many people lose their hearing as they grow older, but they can also lose their hearing through illness, accidents, explosions, or jobs with a lot of constant noise. Some children are born deaf. Doctors don't always know why this happens, but sometimes deafness is **inherited** from one of the parents.

▼ **This diagram shows the inside of a human ear.**

How the ear works

Sound waves go into the **ear** and down a tube called the ear canal. They then cause the **eardrum** to **vibrate**. Next to the eardrum are three little bones called the hammer, the anvil, and the stirrup. They are the smallest bones in the body—all three would fit on a person's little fingernail. These bones pass the vibrations on to the **cochlea**. **Nerves** then carry the sound messages to the brain.

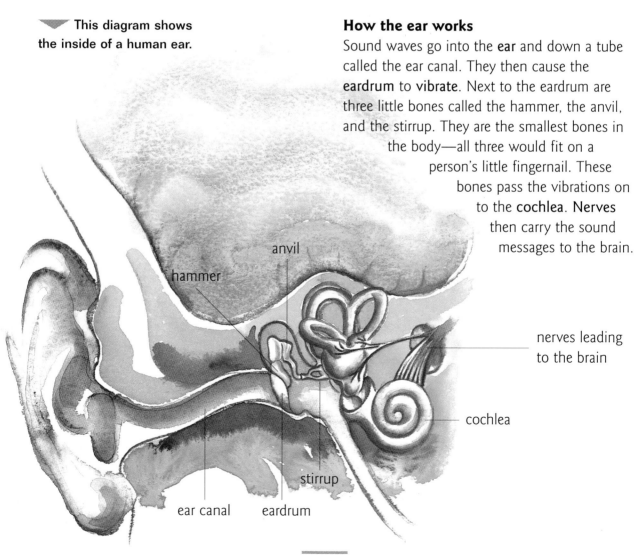

hammer

anvil

nerves leading to the brain

cochlea

stirrup

ear canal   eardrum

Different kinds of deafness

Any part of the ear can be damaged, causing different kinds of deafness. A very loud sound such as an explosion can puncture the eardrum, keeping it from vibrating properly. People who work in noisy jobs often lose their hearing slowly as the nerves in the cochlea are damaged by the constant noise.

▲ Workers wear ear protection so that their hearing isn't damaged by loud machines.

How do we know if a baby is deaf?

Babies can be tested for deafness soon after they are born. Doctors use special equipment to see how the baby's brain reacts to sounds. Deaf people often can't hear consonant sounds such as "s" and "t," which are higher than vowel sounds such as "e" and "o." This makes it very difficult for them to understand speech.

THINK ABOUT

Sound

What is it like to be deaf? People who are hard-of-hearing can hear background noise, but they can't tell what someone is saying to them. It is like listening to loud music through headphones and trying to hear someone talking to you at the same time. People who are very deaf use their other senses instead. They watch people's faces and read their lips. They can also tell a lot by sensing vibrations.

A baby's hearing can be tested in different ways. The baby's response to this squeaky toy gives the doctor an idea of how much the baby can hear.

7

A history of deafness

For hundreds of years, most people thought deaf people were stupid because they couldn't speak properly. No one understood sign language or realized that it was a proper language. Hearing people and deaf people couldn't communicate at all. Before modern **hearing aids** were invented, it was hard to help deaf children learn to speak.

Deaf American settlers
In the 16th century, many English people came to live in America. Some settlers—including a few deaf people—lived on an island called Martha's Vineyard. Over time, the number of deaf people grew, and sign language became a common way of communicating. People slowly came to recognize the usefulness of sign language and the abilities of the deaf.

 **Deaf and hearing people lived together on Martha's Vineyard. The need to work together made all settlers improve ways of communicating with one another.**

Early schools

The first schools for deaf children were set up in the 18th century in Great Britain and Europe. An American named Thomas Gallaudet saw these schools and decided to start a school for deaf children in the United States. He went back to the U.S. with a deaf teacher from France named Laurent LeClerc, who taught American teachers to use sign language. A school was soon set up in Connecticut.

Children learning biology at a special school for deaf children in 1908.

A deaf child in a speech class in the 1940s.
These lessons were very hard for many children.

Banning sign language

In the 19th and early 20th centuries, many people thought that deaf children should learn to speak instead of having a language of their own. Sign language was banned in many schools around the world, and deaf teachers lost their jobs. It was a very sad time for many deaf people because, without sign language, they couldn't learn to read and write properly. Although children were punished for using sign language, they still signed when the teachers weren't looking.

THINK ABOUT

Jobs

Life was very difficult for deaf children who weren't allowed to use sign language. They weren't taught much, and they were given dull jobs working in factories, making shoes, or sewing clothes. These were very noisy jobs, so employers used deaf people, who wouldn't be distracted by all the noise. Most people thought that deaf people couldn't do any other kind of work.

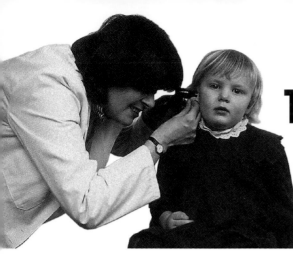

Treatment of deafness

People sometimes see stories in the news about deaf people who have had amazing operations to help them hear again. Although some operations do help people to hear better, only a few people ever have perfect hearing again. But there are ways to prevent deafness or to help people make the most of the hearing they have left.

"Fluid in the ears"

Children sometimes have a kind of ear disorder that doctors call "fluid in the ears." The ears become blocked by fluids that cause a stuffed-up feeling or even earaches. Sometimes this problem is cured by placing a tiny tube inside the ear. "Fluid in the ears" can last a long time, and some children have it again and again.

▶ Most of us have been a little bit deaf at one time or another. Having plugged ears is a very common problem that can be relieved with ear drops. They quickly remove the blockage and ease the pain.

(THINK ABOUT)

Protecting your ears

Some deafness can be prevented if people protect their ears. Many people have hearing problems because they have spent too much time listening to loud music. Objects accidentally poked into an ear can also damage hearing.

Wearing a hearing aid

Hearing aids help some deaf people to hear better by **amplifying** sounds. A hearing aid, which is usually worn behind the ear, has a tiny microphone powered by batteries. A plastic tube goes from the hearing aid to an **earmold** inside the ear. Everyone's ears are shaped differently, so a special mold is made to fit inside the ear. Children, whose ears are still growing, need new molds every few months.

This boy is enjoying a puppet show with a special sign language toy (see page 16). You can see the boy's earmold, the hearing aid, and the wire leading to the batteries.

Operations to help deafness

Eardrums can sometimes be repaired with an operation, and the three bones in the ear can sometimes be replaced with **artificial** bones. People with a badly damaged cochlea may have a **cochlear implant** placed under the skin behind the ear. They wear a tiny microphone that picks up sounds, which are turned into electrical signals by a special box called a speech processor. The signals are then transmitted into the inner ear and passed along the nerves. When the messages reach the brain, they give the sensation of sound.

The part of the cochlear implant behind the ear is the microphone. It picks up sounds and sends them to the round piece on the head, which is a transmitter that sends messages to a receiver inside the head.

At home

Many people wonder if deaf children are able to join in games with their brothers and sisters, or if they are able to understand what is said to them. There are lots of ways to help deaf children be part of a happy family; after all, they can do everything except hear. Families learn how to communicate so that a deaf child can always join activities.

Being part of the family

When there is a deaf person in the family, everyone must remember to include them at all times. Family members often chat while they are preparing a meal or getting ready for school, and a deaf child might find it hard to keep up with the conversation. Everyone should make sure the deaf person knows what is going on. Of course, deaf children should also have a say in such decisions as what to play or eat.

This deaf girl, reading with her mother, is profoundly deaf, which means that she can hardly hear at all, even with a hearing aid.

Learning to be helpful

Deaf people need to be able to see a person to understand what he or she is saying. After tapping them gently on the shoulder to get their attention, it is best to talk to deaf people while standing still. Many people have walked into lampposts because they were talking or signing to a deaf person without looking where they were going.

A person must try to speak clearly when talking to a deaf person.

Deaf children often enjoy playing with colorful toys like this clown and play mat.

Playtime

Deaf babies need lots of toys to keep them interested and **alert**. The best toys are ones that are bright and colorful with plenty of parts to look at and touch, such as the toys in the pictures above. Toys that move or light up when the deaf child makes a sound are good too; they help the child to realize when he is making sounds.

THINK ABOUT

Families

Now imagine what it would be like if your mom or dad were deaf. If they used sign language, you would probably learn to use it too. Many children of deaf parents go on to careers as sign language interpreters. Others may be skilled as actors because of their practice at communicating by using movements, gestures, and facial expressions.

At school

Children use their hearing all the time at school—on the playground, in the lunchroom, and in class. Often, the only quiet time in school is when the teacher tells everyone to stop talking and to concentrate on their work. Deaf children often experience school very differently.

These children go to a school for hearing and deaf students. Some children wear extra-strong hearing aids at school to make sure they can hear everything the teacher says.

Special help for deaf students

About 90 percent of deaf children go to ordinary schools. Some schools have special classes for deaf children to spend part of the day with specially-trained teachers. These classes are very small so that teachers can make sure each child gets the individual attention he needs to learn as much as hearing children. Sometimes teachers wear a microphone so that the students can hear them more clearly.

Schools for deaf children

Some children go to special schools where all the children are deaf and use sign language. Some children prefer these schools because they can all understand each other. If a child lives a long way from the school, he or she may live at school during the week and go home on weekends.

▼ Many students, including deaf children, learn to play musical instruments at school. This deaf girl plays the recorder.

▲ In many special schools, all teachers know how to use sign language. This teacher, who is deaf, "talks" with his deaf students.

Music lessons

Deaf children learn the same subjects at school as hearing children do, including music lessons. Deaf children can play in an orchestra, perform solos, or participate in plays using sign language.

Communication

Deaf babies may have difficulty learning to communicate. They don't speak clearly because they can't hear the noises they are making or the way other people speak. But with the help of sign language, hearing aids, and **lipreading**, deaf children can learn to communicate just as well as hearing children.

The hands of this big puppet can be moved to teach deaf children sign language. The puppet's mouth and tongue can also be moved to show which lip and tongue positions are used to form basic sounds.

Lipreading

Many deaf people learn to lip-read to help them understand what people are saying. Lipreading can be very difficult—not all sounds are easy to see on a person's lips, and many sounds look the same. Look in a mirror and mouth the sounds "f" and "v." They look very similar. Now try the sounds "p," "b," and "m." It is easy to make mistakes trying to lip-read such similar mouth positions.

These deaf teenagers are using sign language.

Queen Victoria learned how to fingerspell so that she could talk to Mrs. Tuffield, a deaf woman who ran the local post office.

Fingerspelling

Words can also be signed using **fingerspelling**. This type of communication, which has a sign for each letter of the alphabet, is easy to learn. British people use two hands for fingerspelling, but people in the U.S. and many other countries use only one hand. A person must know the spoken language of a country to understand its fingerspelling. For example, learning Japanese fingerspelling is impossible if a person doesn't speak any Japanese.

Sign language

Signing looks very complicated, but it is much easier than lipreading once people learn it. Unlike lipreading, which requires a lot of guesswork, signing is a true language.

When people sign, they use their hands and face to communicate meaning. Sign languages are different in almost every country. Just like spoken language, signing varies from place to place; people from different areas of the same country have different accents.

THINK ABOUT
Everyday signs

Can you think of other people who use sign language? During football games, players and coaches sign to each other. Signs are vital to people such as deep sea divers and astronauts, who can't communicate verbally. We use signs every day, such as nodding, waving, and pointing. When people are excited or angry, they often move their hands or bodies with more emphasis.

Out and about

Deafness is often called an invisible disability. On a busy sidewalk, we notice blind people or people in wheelchairs, but we can't see deafness. Usually people don't realize that a person is deaf unless they see her signing to another person. But even then they can't be sure that both people are deaf; perhaps one of them can hear and is using sign language because the other is deaf.

Shopping and traveling

As more people learn sign language, deaf people can communicate easier in places such as stores and restaurants. More public places are now giving deaf people extra help. Many airports, for example, have staff who have been specially trained to communicate with deaf people. Sign language interpreters help deaf people communicate with people who don't know sign language.

A deaf woman (right) uses a sign language interpreter (left) to help at a business meeting.

Using an interpreter

Sign language interpreters can help deaf people in many places. The interpreter listens to what is said and **translates** it into sign language. Interpreters also translate sign language into speech. They work in places such as courts of law, hospitals, and universities.

A sign language interpreter gives deaf people a guided tour of a museum.

Hearing dogs for deaf people

Most people have seen guide dogs helping blind people, but dogs can be trained to help deaf people too. Young hearing dogs spend a year with a foster family to determine if they will be good at working with deaf people. They then spend four months at a training center before they are given to a deaf owner.

Hearing dogs help their owners at home and work. They let their owners know when the phone or doorbell is ringing and even wake them up in the morning when the alarm clock goes off.

This hearing dog, named Kenya, was rescued from a dog pound and is now happily settled with her new family.

THINK ABOUT

Using your eyes

In train stations, airports, and many public places, announcements are made over loudspeakers. Deaf people have to look for written information to tell them when a train is due or if it is delayed. The same information announced over loudspeakers is often displayed on signs or computer screens.

Fun and games

Like many groups that share a common language, deaf people often enjoy being together. There are hundreds of clubs where the deaf can meet to relax or share hobbies. Deaf people also play all kinds of sports. When learning outdoor activities

that require good communication—such as rock climbing, canoeing, or sailing—deaf people need help from someone who can communicate clearly with them.

Brian Kokoruwe, who has competed in the deaf Olympic Games, is one of the fastest deaf 400 m runners in Europe.

Deaf athletics

The deaf Olympic Games, held every four years, are a chance for thousands of deaf people to represent their country. Crowds of people use sign language from all over the world to cheer the athletes on.

Even athletes who are too deaf to hear the starting gun can be great runners. They learn to be so aware of the other runners to their left and right that they spring into action at the same moment as everyone else.

Theater, art, and dance

When deaf people gather to have a good time, they may form a big circle and tell stories or jokes in sign language. Many deaf people enjoy acting and performing songs, dance, or poetry in sign language. Some deaf painters and sculpters use art to express their feelings about deafness. Their unique perspective often helps them create stunning artwork.

This painting by a deaf artist uses bold and colorful shapes to make hearing aids look cheerful and fun.

Evelyn Glennie plays many percussion instruments such as bells and drums.

Making music

Surprisingly, many deaf people love playing musical instruments. Some people who have a little bit of hearing can hear low notes and feel the vibrations of higher notes. Evelyn Glennie is a musician who works all over the world, playing in orchestras and composing music for television and films. She became deaf when she was eight years old, but it did not change her love for music.

THINK ABOUT

Free time

Think about things you enjoy doing and how a deaf person might enjoy them. Could a deaf person fly an airplane or go sky-diving? Although a loss of hearing may seem like a very serious handicap to most people, deaf people can do almost all of the things that hearing people enjoy doing.

Going to work

When young deaf people reach adulthood, they want to work, earn money, have families of their own, and achieve other goals. Deaf people are as intelligent as hearing people and can get an equally good education. But it can still be difficult for them to find the job they want, because employers often think that deaf people will not be able to communicate at work.

All kinds of jobs

Deaf people have a wider choice of careers than many people think. A deaf person might become a writer, computer expert, or laborer. Deaf people can always do a good job as long as everyone understands their needs and makes an effort to communicate with them.

▶ **Many people enjoy careers working outside. This man is deaf and has a job looking after large areas of land in the country.**

Being a journalist

In the past, deaf people were rejected for many jobs because they couldn't use telephones. Today, there are many other ways to keep in touch, such as **fax** and **e-mail**. Melissa, who is deaf, is a journalist who has worked for major magazines such as Vogue. She has a **pager** and a **Minicom** to communicate.

▶ **Melissa regularly visits clothes shows and writes about new styles and fashions.**

Presenting TV programs

Jackie, who is deaf and has a cochlear implant, works as a sign language presenter on a television program. She is also taking classes to be a lawyer.

▲ **Jackie works hard to make time for her studies and her job as a television presenter.**

THINK ABOUT

Having a career

Everyone thinks about the job he or she would like to have someday. Are there any jobs that you think a deaf person couldn't do? Deaf people become lawyers, astronomers, models, and truck drivers. In fact, they can have just about every job you can think of apart from being telephone operators. Deaf people can't be sound engineers in a film crew either, but they can work in film or television.

Amazing inventions

There are many inventions that help deaf people today. Probably the most useful devices are the special telephones that allow deaf people to communicate with anyone else. The first telephone was invented by Alexander Graham Bell in 1876. Bell was very interested in the human voice, in part because his mother and his wife were both deaf. But it wasn't until 100 years later that telephones were invented for deaf people too.

Helping people to hear better

The loop system helps people with hearing aids to hear music or the television. A loop is a wire with a microphone near the source of sound. Deaf people turn a switch on their hearing aid and pick up sound from the microphone. Public places such as theaters, stores, and airports often have loops.

Alarms and warnings

Alarm clocks for deaf people can be attached to a light that flashes or a pad that vibrates when the alarm goes off. Lights in the house can be connected to telephones, smoke alarms, security alarms, and doorbells. When an alarm goes off, the deaf person is alerted by flashing lights.

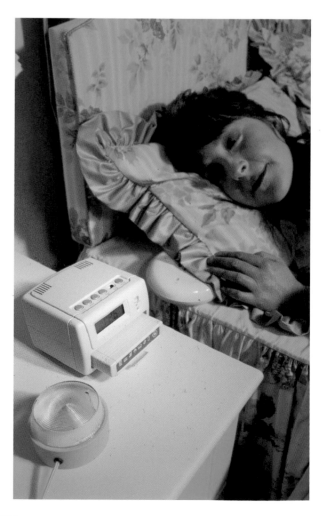

This alarm clock has a light that flashes when the alarm goes off. There is also a round pad under the pillow. The pad vibrates at the same time as the alarm rings, waking the deaf person.

Today, many TV shows have subtitles, or captions. To provide this feature, someone must listen to shows and type in what is said. The words appear at the bottom of the TV screen, often in different colors.

Special telephones

Many deaf people use telephones called **textphones** at home and work. Instead of speaking and listening through the phone, they type and read messages on a screen. Many stores, banks, and public telephones now have Minicoms.

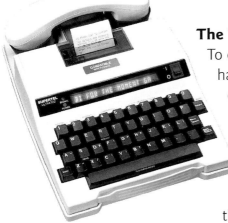

Many deaf people use the textphone. A message is typed on the small screen and sent to someone. It is also printed out.

The Typetalk service

To contact a deaf person who has a textphone, a person can use a telephone service called Typetalk. After an operator types the caller's message and sends it to the deaf person's textphone, the person types a reply and the operator reads it to the caller.

THINK ABOUT

Modern technology

Think about all the equipment we use today, including fax machines and computers. Although they weren't designed specifically for deaf people, they are very useful for people who can't hear. Sending a message by fax or e-mail is a quick and easy way of communicating if you can't speak or listen through a phone. Technology is improving all the time; it might not be long before everyone is using the Internet or communicating over visual telephones.

Famous deaf people

Throughout history, there have been many famous deaf people. The Roman Emperor Hadrian was supposedly so deaf that he had to ride into battle with his hand cupped behind his ear! Some people tried to hide their deafness. For example, Queen Alexandra, the wife of Edward VII, wore elaborate hairstyles and huge hats to cover **ear trumpets** that were designed to look like jewelry.

Ludwig van Beethoven (1770-1827)

Ludwig van Beethoven was a famous composer, pianist, and conductor. From the age of 28, he gradually became deaf. At first he was upset and depressed, but he went on to compose some of his most famous symphonies. By the age of 48, Beethoven was completely deaf.

Deaf artists

There have been many successful deaf artists. Francisco de Goya (1746-1828) was a Spanish painter who became totally deaf after a serious illness. Henri de Toulouse-Lautrec (1864-1901) was a French artist who was **partially** deaf. The English painter Joshua Reynolds (1723-92) lost his hearing in a riding accident. David Hockney (1937-) is a modern artist who wears hearing aids as colorful as the pictures he paints.

This painting is a self-portrait by Joshua Reynolds. He has his hand behind his ear to help him hear better.

As Beethoven became deaf, he cut off communication with those around him, expressing his emotions through music instead.

Thomas Edison (1847-1931)

Thomas Edison is one of the world's most famous inventors. Although he became deaf when he was a boy, Edison went on to invent the light bulb and more than 1,000 devices. He also invented the phonograph, the first device to record and play sounds, even though he couldn't hear it. Edison improved Alexander Graham Bell's early telephone as well.

World leaders

Numerous world leaders have been deaf. Winston Churchill, Great Britain's prime minister during World War II and the early 1950s, didn't want people to know that he was hard-of-hearing. Two other important national leaders, Bill Clinton of the United States and Nelson Mandela of South Africa, are also hard-of-hearing.

▲ Thomas Edison's amazing inventions helped change the world. It's tough to imagine what life would be like without electricity.

(THINK ABOUT)

Fame

Read about other famous deaf people. Did being deaf create problems or stop them from achieving their goals?

▲ Both Nelson Mandela and Bill Clinton wear hearing aids that are small and not easily seen.

Looking to the future

One hundred years ago, there were no hearing aids, and few people understood sign language. There were no special telephones or interpreters to help deaf people in public places. There are many devices available for deaf people today. But how will life change for deaf people in the next 100 years?

New technology

Hearing aids are being improved all the time, and future hearing aids should provide much better sound quality. The newest hearing aids are small enough to fit inside the ear canal. They can't be too small, however, or it would be impossible to use the switches.

Hearing aids are currently being developed that have no switches at all and are **implanted** inside a person's head. Scientists are also trying to program computers to recognize human speech. Perhaps someday, deaf people will have tiny pocket computers that instantly translate speech into writing or signing.

Some people already use tiny hearing aids that fit inside the ear canal. The cable sticks out so that the hearing aid can be pulled out.

Future sign language

Over the last century, deaf people have developed an international sign language so that they can understand people of different nationalities. There may soon be sign language television channels. More and more hearing people are learning to sign; there are even college courses available in sign language and Deaf Studies. The day may come when all children will learn sign language at school.

These children are taking part in a sign language class for hearing and deaf children.

A deaf child from Botswana, Africa, with a special solar-powered hearing aid. It is rechargeable, which means that it doesn't use up expensive batteries.

Could deafness disappear?

Deafness will probably never disappear entirely, but as we learn more about **genes**, it might be possible to help damaged parts of the ear grow again. As doctors and scientists learn more about the ear, they may be able to correct ear problems sooner. As such positive changes come, deaf people worldwide will continue to enjoy more and more opportunities at school, at work, and in the home.

THINK ABOUT
Know the rules

There are several rules of thumb to remember when talking to a deaf person. Make sure there is light on your face so the deaf person can see your mouth and expressions clearly. Either use sign language or gestures and facial expressions to make lipreading easier. Finally, try to speak clearly.

Glossary

alert Aware of surroundings and paying attention.

amplify To make louder. Hearing aids amplify sound for deaf people.

artificial Something that is man-made, not natural.

cochlea A spiral tube, shaped like a snail shell, in the ear. Sound vibrations go through the middle ear and into the cochlea, where they are changed into nerve messages. The messages are then sent to the brain and heard as sound.

cochlear implant A type of hearing aid that can help people who have a damaged cochlea. An implant, put in the person's cochlea, turns sounds to electrical signals and passes them to the brain.

ear The organ that collects sounds. The outer ear is the part that is seen and the ear canal. The middle ear contains three tiny bones. The inner ear sorts out sounds for the brain and includes the cochlea (see diagram on page 6).

eardrum A thin layer of tissue inside the ear that separates the outer ear from the middle ear. Sound vibrates the eardrum.

earmold The part of a hearing aid that fits in the ear.

ear trumpet A long tube that widens at the end. Some people used ear trumpets before modern hearing aids were invented. People held the trumpet to one ear to help them hear what other people were saying.

e-mail A way of sending written messages from one computer to another.

fax A quick way of sending letters or other documents. The paper goes through the fax machine, and the message is sent through a telephone line to another machine, where the page is printed out.

fingerspelling A signing method also called the manual alphabet. Simple hand symbols for each letter of the alphabet are used to spell out words and names.

"fluid in the ears" Thick liquid behind the eardrum that plugs the ear, keeping a person from hearing properly. This problem is often cured with a tiny tube. After a small cut is made in the eardrum to let the liquid drain out, the tube is put in place to let air into the ear and keep it healthy.

genes Parts of cells in the body that make each person different. Babies inherit their genes from their parents.

hearing aid A device that makes sounds louder for people who are partially deaf or hard-of-hearing. Sound is picked up by a microphone and passed into the ear through a small tube. Hearing aids only amplify sounds that the person can already hear, which means that they can't help a person who is totally deaf.

implant To place something inside the body.

inherited Passed down from a parent. Children inherit their physical looks from parents. They can also inherit disabilities such as deafness if they have deaf parents.

lipreading Watching a person's lips to figure out what he or she is saying. Some deaf people learn to lip-read, but a hearing aid is usually used as well to clarify meaning.

Minicom A textphone with a keyboard and a small screen.

nerves Tiny, thin connections that carry messages to the brain from all parts of the body.

pager A small machine that has a screen to display messages. A person speaks the message to a telephone operator or sends typed messages from a textphone.

partially In part but not totally. People with partial deafness have some hearing that can be improved with the use of a good hearing aid.

sign language A method of communication among deaf people that is based on gestures and expressions. It is "spoken" using hand movements and facial expressions. Deaf people all over the world use sign language.

sign language interpreter A person who translates speech into sign language and sign language into speech to help hearing people and deaf people understand each other.

subtitles A written version of the speech and sounds on a television program or video.

textphone A special telephone with a keyboard and a small screen. A deaf person types in a message and sends it to someone else's textphone, where it is displayed on the screen.

translate To hear or read something in one language and change it into another language.

Typetalk A telephone service that lets hearing people and deaf people talk to each other. A telephone operator reads out a textphone message typed by a deaf person. The operator also types out the words spoken by a hearing person for the deaf person to read.

vibrate To move back and forth very quickly. Sounds vibrate inside the ear, allowing us to hear. Vibrations from loud noises can often be felt throughout the body.

Useful addresses

For more information about deafness, contact these organizations or visit their web sites.

Alexander Graham Bell Association for the Deaf
3417 Volta Place NW
Washington, DC 20007
http://www.agbell.org/

American Society for Deaf Children
1820 Tribute Road, Suite A
Sacramento, CA 95815
http://www.deafchildren.org/

Association of Late Deafened Adults
P.O. Box 93075
Rochester, NY 14692
http://www.alda.org/

Better Hearing Institute
5021-B Backlick Road
Annandale, VA 22003
http://www.betterhearing.org/

Canadian Hard of Hearing Association
2435 Holly Lane, Suite 205
Ottawa, ON K1V 7P2
http://www.cyberus.ca/~chhanational/

The Canadian Hearing Society
271 Spadina Road
Toronto, ON M5R 2V3
http://www.chs.ca/home_cont.html

League for Hard of Hearing
71 West 23rd Street, Suite 1805
New York, NY 10010
http://www.lhh.org/

National Association of the Deaf
814 Thayer Ave.
Silver Spring, MD 20910
http://www.nad.org/

Self Help for Hard of Hearing People
7910 Woodmont Ave., Suite 1200
Bethesda, MD 20814
http:www.shhh.org/

Index